Irish Family History
A Beginners' Guide

Stuart A. Raymond

THE FAMILY HISTORY PARTNERSHIP

Published by
The Family History Partnership
57 Bury New Road
Ramsbottom, Bury
Lancashire BL0 0BZ

First published 2016

ISBN: 978 1 906280 56 7

Printed in the United Kingdom by Henry Ling Limited
at the Dorset Press, Dorchester, Dorset, DT11 1HD

Contents

Front cover picture

Emigrants Leave Ireland, by Henry Doyle, 1868.
Courtesy of Wikimedia.

Acknowledgements

I am grateful for the help of Sherry Irvine and Richard Ratcliffe, both of whom read my text and saved me from errors – although any remaining are of course my responsibility. My thanks too to Bob Boyd, who has seen the book through the press, and to the other members of the Family History Partnership for their support.

Abbreviations

GRO   General Registry Office

IFHoW   Raymond, Stuart A. *Irish Family History on the Web.* 4th ed. Family
           History Partnership, 2016.

LDS   Latter Day Saints

Maxwell   Maxwell, Ian. *Tracing your Irish ancestors.* Pen & Sword, 2008.

NAI   National Archives of Ireland

NLI   National Library of Ireland

Grenham   Grenham, John. *Tracing your Irish Ancestors.* 4th ed. Gill &
           Macmillan, 2012.

PRONI   Public Record Office of Northern Ireland

TNA   The National Archives [UK]

Introduction

Tracing family history is a fascinating pursuit, which can be very personal: you are trying to trace people without whom you might not exist. Genealogy is rather like a jigsaw puzzle, but there is no box for the pieces, some of which are likely to be missing. The sources you must use were not written in order to assist your research. You must compare those sources with each other, and assess the value of the evidence they provide. But genealogy is not necessarily a lone task. There are many sources of help. Archivists and librarians can provide professional assistance; family history societies are there to help their members; internet forums enable individual family historians to contact each other. All of them may be able to assist with specific problems encountered in your research. And the advent of the internet means that research has become much easier than it was in the past – despite the fact that many Irish sources have been lost. It should be possible to trace your Irish ancestors at least as far back as the nineteenth century, and perhaps much earlier if you are lucky.

Ireland has had a troubled past. Invaded by Norman kings, and ruled by an alien elite, its Celtic inhabitants frequently rebelled; their loyalty was always suspect. Protestantism was merely an alien imposition, never accepted by the majority of Irish. In the sixteenth and seventeenth centuries, Roman Catholics were subjected to extensive dispossession; much property was seized from them and granted to 'protestant' settlers, many of them Presbyterian Scots (especially in Ulster). In 1801, the Irish Parliament was abolished, and Irish Members were elected to the United Kingdom Parliament. The demand for Home Rule, however, became increasingly strong in the nineteenth century, despite the predominance of the Presbyterian church in Ulster. The Easter Rebellion of 1916 and subsequent risings eventually led to Irish independence in 1922, although Northern Ireland remained within the United Kingdom.

This history is reflected in the fragmentary nature of the surviving records. Fortunately, the civil registers of births, marriages, and deaths, survived the struggle for Irish independence and the subsequent civil war. The latter conflict did, however, lead to the destruction of the Irish Public Record Office in 1922. Much was lost. For genealogists, the worst losses were the probate records, and those Church of Ireland parish registers which had been deposited.

Despite this disaster, much still survives. Family historians need to be aware of the importance of religious divisions, which meant that the Church of Ireland (the established church until the late nineteenth century) has never been the most important denomination conducting baptisms, marriages and burials. That position was held by the Roman Catholics, whose registers do survive (although rarely before the 1820s). In Ulster, the Presbyterians were more important, although, again, registers prior to 1800 are scarce. Other denominations – Methodists, Quakers, Huguenots, etc., have also been active. Despite the destruction of 1922, many sources of information on baptisms, marriages and burials prior to the introduction of civil registration have survived, at least for the late eighteenth and early nineteenth centuries. It is important to identify all the denominations which were active in the area where your ancestors lived, and to discover whether any registers survive. It is also important to check any surviving Church of Ireland registers, irrespective of whether your ancestors belonged to that denomination. Only marriages conducted by Church of Ireland clergymen were legally valid.

Other records are also important. Valuation Records, including Griffith's Primary Valuation, the tithe applotment books, and other valuations, help to make up for the fact that nineteenth century census records are either fragmentary or have been totally destroyed. The census returns for 1901 and 1911 are, however available, and will enable you to identify your ancestors at the beginning of the twentieth century. A wide range of other minor sources are also available: occupational records, the Catholic qualification rolls, and freeholders' lists, are amongst the numerous sources where you might be able to find titbits of information that will help grow your family tree. This book is intended merely as an introduction to such sources; there are many records not mentioned here that you are likely to discover as your research proceeds.

Preliminaries

Family historians are dependent on original sources, printed books, and the internet. There is a tendency to assume that nowadays everything is available on the internet. It is not. Yes, a huge amount of information is available online, and research is much easier as a consequence. But the majority of documents held in record offices are not online, nor likely to be in the immediate future. Documents which have not been digitised for the internet may be just as relevant to your research as those which are online. So you may still need to visit record offices. There are also many books which may contain useful information not available on the internet. And the internet cannot replace the information on your family history which your relatives may be able to supply. The first step in genealogical research is to ask your relatives.

When you commence your research, you may find it useful to join a family history society (see below, p.13) or an internet discussion forum. Many family history society websites have lists of their members' interests; it is worth adding your interests to these lists, as you may find others researching the same lines as yourself. Discussion forums enable you to seek advice from others who may be more knowledgeable than you. Numerous Irish discussion forums and mailing lists are listed by:

- Genealogy Resources on the Internet: Ireland Mailing Lists
  www.rootsweb.ancestry.com/~jfuller/gen_mail_country-unk-irl.html

Useful information may also be found in family history magazines, such as:

- Irish Lives Remembered Genealogy Magazine
  www.irishlivesremembered.ie
- Irish Roots Magazine
  www.irishrootsmedia.com

For an index to articles appearing in over 150 magazines, compiled by NLI, see the database listed below, p.10.

If you need to visit a library or record office, remember to check their opening times before you go. And bear in mind that many of them close annually for stock taking. Their websites should give details. Don't travel hundreds of miles to a record office only to find it closed!

Be aware of the differences between original sources, transcripts, indexes, and printed books. It is always best to consult the original source if you can. A digitised online image is generally just as acceptable, unless the handwriting is too faded to read without an ultraviolet light, or the camera misses a page. A transcription should be an exact copy of the original document, word for word, letter for letter. But it is only as good as the transcriber; if he is 95% accurate he is doing well. Most transcripts miss something, very likely the information you seek. An index is merely a list of terms indicating where they can be found in the original manuscript; it does not necessarily give all the information found in the original document.

If you discover relevant information, write it down! None of us have perfect memories. And always cite your sources. You may need to check them again. If you have identified information on the internet, do not just cite the webhost, eg Ancestry, or Find My Past; record the information that will enable you to find the actual document again, eg bibliographical details (minimally author, title, date, & page no.) of printed books, details of record offices & their reference numbers for original sources. If you need to, you should then be able to find the source again in a library, in the record office, or even on a different webhost. More is said about sources on the internet below.

Libraries and Archives

The importance of consulting original sources where you can has already been emphasised. Most of these are held in either the NAI, or the PRONI. Both of these institutions have websites containing a range of research guides, a catalogue of their holdings, and a number of useful databases. Visit:

- National Archives of Ireland
  www.nationalarchives.ie

- Public Record Office of Northern Ireland
  www.nidirect.gov.uk/proni

A comprehensive collection of Irish books is held by:

- National Library of Ireland
  www.nli.ie

NLI also holds numerous journals relating to Ireland, together with microfilms of Irish manuscripts from over 1,000 libraries. These are indexed in:

- Sources: a National Library of Ireland Database for Irish Research
  http://sources.nli.ie

The Genealogical Office is now a part of NLI. It holds records of heraldic visitations, plus many pedigrees, and a range of other sources, for example, Betham's extracts from Prerogative Court wills. Most are indexed by the database just mentioned. For details, consult Grenham, and:

- Office of the Chief Herald
  www.nli.ie/en/intro/heraldry-introduction.aspx

A significant collection of books on Irish history and genealogy is held in Belfast by:

- Linen Hall Library
  www.linenhall.com

The records of the Church of Ireland are held by:

- Representative Church Body Library
  www.ireland.anglican.org/library

Innumerable parish registers, and a vast range of other sources have been microfilmed, and are available through the local Family History Centres of the Latter Day Saints Family History Library. Its website also has numerous advice pages and a number of useful databases (some of which have already been mentioned). See:

- Family Search
  https://familysearch.org

A number of local libraries and record offices hold relevant sources. Their websites cannot all be listed here, but see, for example:
- Clare County Library
  www.clarelibrary.ie
- Cork City and County Archives
  www.corkarchives.ie
- Limerick Archives
  www.limerick.ie/archives

For a detailed listing of Irish repositories, visit:
- The National Archives of Ireland: Related agencies in Ireland and worldwide
  www.nationalarchives.ie/visit-us/related-agencies-in-ireland-and-
  worldwide

It should also be noted that many large reference libraries throughout the English speaking world – for example, the State Library of Victoria in Melbourne, or the Library of Congress in Washington – have substantial collections relating to Irish genealogy.

The Internet

As already noted, a huge amount of genealogical information is now available on the internet. This includes:
- Basic genealogical guidance
- Sources: digitised images of both original sources and of printed books; also transcripts and indexes
- Details of Institutions such as libraries, societies, and archive repositories
- General information on the historical and geographical background, including gazetteers
- Lists of surnames currently being researched
- Discussion forums
- Pages for particular families

Much useful information, together with links to various other genealogical websites, is provided by:
- Genuki Ireland
  www.genuki.org.uk/big/irl

Genuki provides general pages on Ireland as a whole, with separate pages for each county, and also pages for many individual parishes. County pages are also provided by:

- Ireland Genweb
  www.irelandgenweb.com

A number of blogs enable us to keep up to date with what is happening in Irish genealogy. The most useful of these is probably:

- Irish Genealogy News
  www.irishgenealogynews.com

The quality of the information provided by Internet sites is not necessarily always as good as it should be. As a rough rule of thumb, you can trust the advice offered on the websites of major institutions such as record offices and libraries. They are more likely to be accurate than websites provided by private individuals. Some of the latter are excellent, but others are dire. Bear in mind that many webmasters are not experienced genealogists, and that they may not have the resources needed to check data entry thoroughly.

The accuracy of digitised images, transcripts, and indexes, has already been discussed. You should always try to verify the information that they provide. That task is not always made easy by some of the major web hosts. You always need to be aware of where information comes from, in order to determine the value of the evidence provided. That is why you should not trust the hype of commercial hosts, who frequently present you with a search box, and invite you to 'search here', without making it clear what it is that they are actually inviting you to search. For example, Find My Past's Irish civil registration indexes mentioned below p.18 are presumably the same as those used by FamilySearch – but they do not state the source of their information. Details of the sources covered by Ancestry can be found from its front page – but only if you scroll down and press a barely noticeable button. Always ask, what is the origin of the information?

Despite these strictures, and unless you live close to major institutions such as NAI or PRONI, you will almost certainly need to use commercial web hosts. They have digitised a huge array of sources, many of which are noted below. A search which might have taken months in pre-internet days may now only take a few minutes. The most important commercial hosts are:

- Ancestry
  www.ancestry.co.uk
- Find My Past
  www.findmypast.ie
- World Vital Records
  www.worldvitalrecords.com

A free site hosting 22 Irish databases is provided by:
- Family Search
https://familysearch.org

For Ulster, many small databases are hosted by:
- Ulster Historical Foundation
www.ancestryireland.com
(click "Family Records')

There are numerous smaller database hosts. These include the county centres of the Irish Family History Foundation (see p.15). Another example, hosting many records from Co. Clare, is provided by:
- Clare Genealogy and Family History
www.clarelibrary.ie/eolas/coclare/genealogy/genealog.htm

A detailed listing of Irish family history websites is provided by:
- Raymond, Stuart A. *Irish family history on the web.* 4th ed. Family History Partnership, 2015.

Numerous Irish sites can also be identified on:
- Cyndi's List of Genealogical Sites on the Internet
http://cyndislist.com

Family History Societies

Family history societies are valuable sources of help. Most issue regular newsletters, conduct meetings, and undertake transcription or indexing of sources from their local area. The latter are frequently published and available for purchase. Alternatively, they may be available online. Society libraries also hold numerous genealogy related books. By consulting Societies' lists of members' interests, you may be able to make contact with others researching the same lines. Full details of their activities are given on their websites, which frequently also include detailed information relating to local resources. Most Irish societies are members of the Council of Irish Genealogical Organisations (CIGO) **www.cigo.ie**, whose website lists their webpages.

Surnames

Genealogical research depends heavily on the existence of hereditary surnames. Bear in mind that these have evolved over the centuries, and have not remained constant in either spelling or pronunciation. Irish names in particular were affected by the fact that many of the clerks who wrote them down could only speak

English; hence, for example, O Dubhthaight became O'Duffy. It was only in the nineteenth century that spellings became standardised, so you do need to look out for alternative spellings of the surnames you are interested in. There are many guides to Irish surnames; the most comprehensive, giving the origins of over 26,000 names, is available on CD:

- Grenham, John. *Guide to Irish surnames*. CD. Eneclann, 2003.

Administrative Areas

Genealogical sources were usually created within a specific administrative area, whether that was a Province, a County, a barony, a townland, a diocese, a civil or ecclesiastical parish, or a poor law union. You therefore need to be aware of how these divisions related to each other. For secular purposes, Ireland was divided into provinces, each of which was sub-divided into several counties, then into baronies, and then into civil parishes. Each parish usually has several townlands. There are c.62,000 townlands in Ireland. There were many changes in Townland boundaries in the 1830s. A guide to these changes is provided by *Handran's Townlands in Poor law Unions*. This is downloadable from **www.eneclann.ie/acatalog/Archive_CD_Books_Ireland.html**.

For ecclesiastical purposes, the island was also divided into provinces, each of which was divided into dioceses and parishes. However, the dioceses and parishes of the Church of Ireland (Anglican), and of the Roman Catholic Church, are quite different. Currently, the Church of Ireland has two provinces and twelve dioceses; the Roman Catholic church has four provinces and twenty-six dioceses. Anglican parishes were used for secular as well as ecclesiastical government: the relief of poverty and the provision of soldiers were two of its responsibilities. Modern civil parish boundaries were originally based on Church of Ireland parish boundaries, although there have been many changes in the last two centuries. Roman Catholic parishes are general smaller than those of the Church of Ireland, but congregations are much larger. Many changes to their boundaries have also taken place, especially in the nineteenth century.

The various sources which you need to consult were created within this framework. For example, parish registers of baptisms, marriages and burials, record vital events which occurred within the parish. Wills made in the diocese were proved in diocesan courts. The baronies (abolished in 1898) were used for compiling land surveys and early censuses. Later enumerations were based on poor law unions. Townlands were the smallest units used in Griffith's Valuation and in the Tithe Applotment books. Bear in mind when you identify a place name in your sources that it is not necessarily a parish – it could equally be a townland, a barony, or merely a hamlet.

For a more detailed explanation of administrative areas, visit:
- Guide To Irish Land Division
  www.ballybegvillage.com/land_division.html

If you have identified the townland you are interested in, you can easily identify the various administrative divisions into which it falls by consulting the *General Alphabetical Index to the Townlands and Towns, parishes and Baronies of Ireland*, which was published with every census. A copy, for the census year 1861, is available at **www.dippam.ac.uk/eppi/documents/14424/page/372656**.

Civil Registration of Births, Marriages, and Deaths
Civil registration of protestant and civil marriages began on 1ˢᵗ April 1845. Mixed marriages of Catholics and non-Catholics were also recorded, but Catholic marriages were excluded. Roman Catholics objected to the registration of marriages conducted by their priests. That objection was eventually overcome, and all marriages were registered from 1ˢᵗ January 1864. From that date, births and deaths were also registered.

The original registers were kept by district registrars, who still hold them. For a detailed listing of the registration districts in which they operated, see:
- Registration Districts of Ireland: An Alphabetical List of the Registration Districts of Ireland with Details of Counties, Sub Districts, and Adjacent Districts / Michael J. Thompson
  http://genealogyresearch.org.uk/IRL_RegistrationDistricts1871.pdf
  See also *Handran's Townlands*, above, p.14.

District Registrars made quarterly returns to the Irish General Register Office, **www.welfare.ie/en/Pages/General-Register-Office.aspx**, which was formerly in Dublin, but is now in Roscommon. In 1922, a separate General Register Office for Northern Ireland **www.nidirect.gov.uk/gro** was established. Both offices hold indexes for pre 1922 registers (see below). The original registers are not open to public inspection; it is necessary to consult the indexes and purchase certificates (or photocopies in the Irish GRO) in order to obtain the information in them. Note, however, that LDS does hold some microfilm copies of the original registers. These can be obtained through LDS branch libraries. For details, visit **https:// familysearch.org/wiki/en/Ireland_Civil_Registration-_Vital_Records**

Civil Birth Registers
Irish civil registration of births commenced on 1st January 1864. The information in the registers includes:
- date and place of birth
- forename(s)

- sex
- father's forename(s), surname and dwelling place
- mother's forename(s), surname and maiden surname
- father's rank or profession
- signature, qualification and residence of informant
- date of registration
- signature of registrar
- baptismal name, if added after registration of birth, and date.

Civil Marriage Registers
The Irish civil marriage registers commenced on 1st April 1845, although marriages conducted by Roman Catholic priests were not included until 1st January 1864. The information included provides:
- date of marriage
- forenames and surnames of bride and groom
- ages
- condition (i.e. bachelor, widow, etc.)
- rank or professions
- residence(s) at time of marriage
- fathers' forenames and surnames
- ranks or professions of fathers
- church where the marriage was performed
- names of two witnesses
- name of celebrant.

Civil Death Registers
Civil registers of deaths commenced on 1st January 1864. The information in them includes:
- date and place of death
- forename(s) and surname
- sex
- marital status
- age
- rank, profession or occupation
- certified cause of death and duration of illness
- signature, qualification and residence of informant
- when registered

GRO Indexes

There are two official sites where some of the information in the registers can be accessed online. For the Republic of Ireland, visit:

- Irish Genealogy
  http://www.irishgenealogy.ie/en
  This includes indexes to births over 100 years old, indexes to marriages over 75 years old and indexes to deaths over 50 years old. It provides much more information than the commercial indexes listed below, although it is still necessary to obtain certificates if the full information in the registers is to be obtained. It also provides a unique Group Registration ID reference for each entry, which can be used to obtain certificates.

Northern Ireland is covered by:

- Research family history at the General Register Office NI (GRONI)
  www.nidirect.gov.uk/information-and-services/family-history-heritage-and-museums/research-family-history-general
  This includes birth records over 100 years old, marriage records over 75 years old, and death records (including World War II death records) over 50 years old. This site includes digitised images of the original registers.

Computerised indexes for more recent registrations are available in both Roscommon and Belfast, but are not currently available online. Details of GRO register entries can be obtained from the appropriate GRO in Roscommon or Belfast. In Roscommon, it is possible to obtain either a photocopy of the original register, or a certificate. For genealogical purposes, the former is both preferable, since it avoids any error in copying, and is also cheaper. In Belfast, certificates only are available. It is also possible to obtain certificates from district registrars (see below).

Older indexes, some of which have been digitised, are also available. Irish GRO indexes up to 1877 were annual; thereafter they were quarterly, except for births, which were indexed annually from 1903. These indexes record names and registration districts, together with volume and page numbers. Birth entries from 1903 give mothers' maiden names. The indexes for 1864-1958 (1959 for Northern Ireland) have been transcribed by the LDS Family History Library, and are free online, although there are a few gaps, and mothers' maiden names are not indexed. Visit:

Ireland Civil Registration Indexes, 1864-1958
https://familysearch.org/search/collection/1408347
(Excludes Northern Ireland post-1922).

These older indexes are also available for a fee on both Find My Past **www. findmypast.ie**, and on Ancestry **www.ancestry.co.uk**. The search engines provided by these hosts enable much more detailed searching than is available on the Family Search website, and may therefore be worth the subscription. Note that these indexes *do not* record all the information in the registers. Rather, they provide you with the information you need to order a certificate. When you find a relevant entry, you will need to note the surname, the year of the event, the Registration District or Poor Law Union where the event was registered, the volume number, and the page number. If the entry is dated between 1878 and 1902 you will also need to note the quarter in which the event took place. This is also needed after 1902 if the event was a marriage or death. Note that this information is not required if you are using the two official sites mentioned above. For a more detailed account of civil registration, visit:

- Irish Genealogy Toolkit: Using Irish Civil Registration Indexes
  www.irish-genealogy-toolkit.com/irish-civil-registration-indexes.html

District Registrars & the Irish Family History Foundation

District registrars are also able to issue certificates. Bear in mind that the registers of District Registrars are the originals from which the GRO registers were copied. The evidence of the former are therefore to be preferred. Indexes to many of their registers have been compiled by some Irish Family History Foundation centres. These centres are listed at **www.rootsireland.ie**. Note that some centres also offer indexes to sources other than civil registration records.

For the addresses of district registrars, visit:

- Health Service Executive: Sonraí Teagmhála Oifigí Áitiúil: Local Office Contact Detail
  www.hse.ie/eng/services/list/1/bdm/contactus/
  Registrars_of_Births_Deaths_and_Marriages.html
- District Registrars in Northern Ireland
  www.nidirect.gov.uk/contacts/district-registrars-northern-ireland

Other Civil Indexes & Registers

The two GROs also hold a number of other useful registers. These include (with dates of commencement):

Belfast

- Marine births and deaths, 1922
- Adopted children, 1931
- War Deaths, 1939-1948
- Consulate record of births, marriages and deaths overseas, 1922

Roscommon
- Adopted children 1953
- Births and deaths at sea 1864 (deaths to 1921 only)
- Consulate records of Irish births and deaths overseas

The LDS also holds microfilmed copies of some actual registers, which can be borrowed through their branch libraries. Their holdings include:
- Births (all Ireland) 1864-1881; 1900-1913; 1930-55 (to 1959 for Northern Ireland)
- Marriages All Ireland 1845-1870; Northern Ireland 1922-1959
- Deaths All Ireland 1864-1870 (also available online at **https://familysearch.org/search/collection/1584965**)
- Deaths, Northern Ireland 1922-1959

More information is provided by:
- Ireland Civil Registration
https://familysearch.org/learn/wiki/en/
Ireland_Civil_Registration-_Vital_Records

- A Guide to the General Register Office of Ireland: Research in the General Register Office, and Overseas Applications
http://homepage.eircom.net/%257Eseanjmurphy/gro/research.htm
- Irish Civil Registration
www.irish-genealogy-toolkit.com/Irish-civil-registration.html

For a detailed guide to Irish civil registration, consult:
- Blumson, Catherine. *Civil Registration of Births, Deaths and Marriages in Ireland: A Practical Approach.* Ulster Historical Foundation, 1996.
See also *IFHoW* for a listing of numerous birth, marriage, and death websites.

Church Registers of Baptisms, Marriages, and Burials
In order to trace births, marriages and deaths prior to civil registration, it is normally necessary to consult parish registers of baptisms, marriages and burials, which were compiled by Roman Catholic, Church of Ireland, Presbyterian, and other clergy. These continued to be kept after the commencement of civil registration, so they can also be used as an alternative source of information to the civil registers. There are two extensive listings of surviving registers from all denominations:

- Ryan, James G., ed. *Irish Church Records*. 2nd ed. Flyleaf Press, 2001.
- Mitchell, Brian. *A Guide to Irish Parish Registers*. Baltimore: Genealogical Publishing Company, 1998 (2009 reprint).

Numerous registers have been transcribed, indexed, and/or digitised for the internet. For example, a useful collection of Church of Ireland and Roman Catholic registers from Carlow, Cork & Ross, Dublin, and Kerry, is provided by Irish Genealogy **www.irishgenealogy.ie**. Many microfilms of Irish registers are held by the Family History Library **https://familysearch.org**. Numerous online transcripts and indexes can be identified through Genuki Ireland, **www.genuki.org.uk/big/irl**, Ireland Genweb **www.irelandgenweb.com**, and in *IFHoW*. For an extensive list of Northern Irish registers from all denominations held by PRONI (including some microfilms), visit:

- An Irish Genealogical Source: A Guide to Church Records
  www.nidirect.gov.uk/sites/default/files/publications/
  Guide_to_church_records.pdf

Church of Ireland Registers

Reference has already been made to the loss of Church of Ireland registers in the 1922 destruction of the Irish Public Record Office. Fortunately, some registers had been copied before the destruction, and others had not been deposited.

Although Church of Ireland adherents formed a relatively small proportion of the population, its registers recorded many marriages and burials of members of other denominations. It was the established church, and in theory only marriages conducted by its clergy were legally valid.

The information given in Church of Ireland registers is generally not extensive. Baptismal records include the name of the child and its parents. Marriage entries may give merely the names of the parties. Burial entries usually give just the name, the age, and the townland. More extensive information may be found in banns registers, in the rare cases where these still exist. Those which survive may be held in a variety of different places. The Representative Church Body Library, NAI, and PRONI, have good collections. Some registers are still held by local churches. For a full listing of all surviving Church of Ireland registers, visit:

- Table Of Church Of Ireland Parish Registers Throughout Ireland (Baptisms, Marriages, Burials & copies)
  http://ireland.anglican.org/cmsfiles/pdf/AboutUs/library/registers/
  IParishRegistersTable.pdf

An increasing number are available in digitised format at:

- Church of Ireland: Online Parish Records
  http://ireland.anglican.org/about/168

Before a marriage could take place, banns had to be proclaimed in the parish church three times, unless a marriage licence had been obtained from the bishop. Applicants for a licence were required to enter a marriage bond to indemnify the grantor if the details provided proved to be incorrect. These bonds did not survive the destruction of 1922, but indexes to them did, and are now available online:

- Ireland Diocesan and Prerogative Marriage Licence Bonds Indexes 1623-1866
  http://search.findmypast.com/search-world-records/ireland-diocesan-and-prerogative-marriage-licence-bonds-indexes-1623-1866

Ecclesiastical records include far more than just registers of baptisms, marriages and burials. For a full discussion of Church of Ireland records, see:

- Refaussé, Raymond. *Church of Ireland records.* Irish Academic Press, 2006.

Roman Catholic Registers

The majority of Irishmen were Roman Catholics. Sadly, few of their pre-nineteenth century registers survive. Baptisms and marriages are recorded more frequently than burials; burial registers in southern counties are rare. Baptismal entries are likely to record the names of children and their parents (including mothers' maiden names), together with the names of godparents. There was little point in Roman Catholics keeping marriage registers during the eighteenth century, since marriages conducted by their priests were not legally valid (although in practice legality was sometimes ignored). Most Roman Catholic marriage registers date from the 1820s or later, after emancipation. Entries in these registers vary, but are likely to include dates of marriages, names of parties, and the names of witnesses. Additional information, such as addresses and occupations, may sometimes be supplied.

Grenham provides a useful printed guide to surviving Catholic registers. Those held by NLI have been digitised; visit:

- Catholic Parish Registers at NLI
  http://registers.nli.ie

This site includes a full listing of available registers. It also includes digitised images of the registers themselves, which you can browse through. It does not, however, include indexes. They are available on two commercial hosts:

- Ireland, Catholic Parish Registers, 1655-1915
  http://search.ancestry.co.uk/search/db.aspx?dbid=61039
- Find My Past: Irish Parish Records: Catholic Parish Registers
  www.findmypast.co.uk/irish-parish-records

For Northern Ireland, most Roman Catholic registers held by PRONI have been microfilmed; see the listing of registers held by PRONI mentioned above, p.20. Indexes to PRONI registers are included in the two commercial websites just mentioned.

Presbyterian Registers
The Presbyterians are mostly descended from Scottish settlers; they were (and still are) concentrated in Northern Ireland. They founded churches wherever there were sufficient numbers of Presbyterians to form a congregation. Early Presbyterians are frequently found in Church of Ireland registers. Presbyterian registers tend to start much later than those of the Church of Ireland, although they contain much the same information.

Most Presbyterian registers are available on microfilm at PRONI. Many original registers are held by the Presbyterian Historical Society **www.presbyterianhistoryireland.com** in Belfast. In the Republic, most Presbyterian records are still in church custody. Lists of Presbyterian registers are included in the general lists mentioned above, p.20.

Quaker Registers
The Quakers had c.150 Meetings throughout Ireland by 1750. Their Monthly Meetings maintained registers of births (not baptisms), marriages and deaths. These are held by the Friends Historical Library **http://quakers-in-ireland.ie/historical-library** in Dublin, and, for Northern Ireland, by the Archives Committee of the Ulster Quarterly Meeting. Grenham lists available registers. Microfilm copies are available in NAI, NLI, and (for Northern Ireland) PRONI.

For other Quaker records, which include Meeting minutes, records of Sufferings, school and charity records, replies to queries, *etc.*, see:
- Hutton, B.G. *Guide to Irish Quaker Records, 1654-1860.* Irish Manuscripts Commission, 1967. Viewable online at:
  www.irishmanuscripts.ie/servlet/Controller?action=digitisation_backlist

Methodist Registers
Methodists remained within the Church of Ireland, and hence had no separate registers, until 1816. Thereafter, Wesleyan Methodists were authorised to celebrate the sacraments, and kept their own registers. This decision was the occasion of schism; the Primitive Wesleyans remained affiliated with the Church of Ireland. There were a number of other minor denominations: the Primitive Methodists, the Methodist New Connexion, and the Wesleyan Methodist Association.

Most Wesleyan Methodist registers record baptisms and marriages only; burials were mostly in Church of Ireland cemeteries. The information in these registers is similar to that in Church of Ireland registers. Wesleyan registers are mainly still in church custody, although the Methodist Historical Society of Ireland holds an increasing number. Microfilms of many Northern Ireland registers are available at PRONI. Some Irish Family History Foundation centres (see p18) have databases of Methodist records.

Useful information on Methodist registers, together with databases of ministers (in progress), and histories of chapels, can be viewed at:
- Methodist Historical Society of Ireland
  http://methodisthistoryireland.org

Huguenot Registers
A number of Huguenot registers were lost in 1922. However, four volumes of transcripts from Dublin and Portarlington had been published by the Huguenot Society of London **www.huguenotsociety.org.uk** before the destruction. These are still available in libraries, and can be purchased on CD. For a general guide to sources for Irish Huguenots, c.1660-1760, visit the Brigham Young University's *Family Historian* page:
- Researching Huguenot Settlers in Ireland
  http://scholarsarchive.byu.edu/byufamilyhistorian/vol6/iss1/9

Monumental Inscriptions and Cemeteries
Memorials are invaluable sources for family historians. Some are very laconic, with just a name and a date; others may enable you to construct a family tree for several generations . Sometimes, gravestones for different members of the same family are grouped together. If you know where your ancestors came from, it is well worthwhile to visit the local graveyards.

Many transcripts of memorial inscriptions, some compiled by family history societies, have been deposited in libraries and record offices, or used to compile internet databases (see the directories listed on p.13). For some useful advice from the Latter Day Saints, visit:
- Ireland Cemeteries
  https://familysearch.org/learn/wiki/en/Ireland_Cemeteries
There are numerous gravestone databases; one of the largest, with 400,000+ records, is:
- Ireland's Gravestone Index
  www.irish-world.com/gravestones/index.cfm

Inscriptions from over 3,400 Irish cemeteries are included in:
- Find a Grave
http://findagrave.com

Indexes to many Irish cemetery registers are included in:
- Interment.net
http://interment.net/ireland/index.htm
For inscriptions from Ulster, see:
- History from Headstones
www.historyfromheadstones.com/index.php?home

For a collection of published transcripts identifying over 67,000 people, see:
- Cantwell, Brian J. *Cantwell's Memorials of the Dead: The Collected Works.* Irish Memorial Inscriptions 2. CD. Eneclann, [20—]. These volumes are also available on Find My Past.

Cantwell continued the work of the Association for the Preservation of the Memorials of the Dead in Ireland. It published annual journals from 1888 to 1934, incorporating numerous transcripts of inscriptions. Many of these are digitised at **https://archive.org**. Numerous other transcripts and indexes of inscriptions on the internet are listed by *IFHoW.*

Lists of Names

Lists of names are invaluable sources of information for family historians. In general, they were not compiled for genealogical purposes, but nevertheless may include valuable information such as addresses and occupations. A wide variety of lists of names are available. The census is the most important, as it aimed to provide a comprehensive listing of the population, and to identify relationships within household. The Tithe Applotment Books and Griffith's Valuation, which were compiled several decades apart, serve as valuable substitutes where censuses are not available; both identify heads of households, although the tithe records are only available in rural areas, and do not include those too poor to pay tithe. Many other lists of names are available; some of the more extensive are mentioned below. These may enable you to establish your ancestors' presence in a specific place at a specific time, and give you clues for further research.

The Census

Census records are invaluable sources for family historians, since they should identify everyone in the country at a specific point in time. Unfortunately, in

Ireland only the censuses taken in 1901 and 1911 are reasonably complete. There was no census taken in 1921. Most of the earliest censuses have been destroyed, although a few fragments for 1821-51 are available. In the 1821 and 1831 fragments, only heads of households are named. The returns for 1901 and 1911 include name, age, sex, relationship to head of the household, religion, occupation, marital status, county or country of birth. In 1911, married women were also asked to state the number of years they had been married, the number of their children born alive, and the number still living.

The basic unit used in compiling the census was the townland or street. These were arranged within electoral divisions, and then within counties. For full details of these records, together with digitised images of the original returns, visit:

- Census of Ireland 1901/1911 and Census fragments and substitutes, 1821-51
  www.census.nationalarchives.ie

All surviving 19th century census fragments can also be searched at FindMyPast **www.findmypast.ie/articles/world-records/full-list-of-the-irish-family-history-records/census-land-and-substitutes/ireland-census-1821-1851**. The LDS holds microfilms of these fragments; for details, visit **https://familysearch.org/wiki/en/Ireland_Census_fragments_available_at_the_Family_History_Library**.

Portions of censuses are also available on many other websites. They are listed by *IFHoW*.

When old age pensions were introduced at the beginning of the twentieth century, many did not have proof of age which was required in order to apply. In these instances, the government searched the 1841 and 1851 censuses in order to prove the ages of claimants. They recorded the information they found in the census on special search forms. These survive, and thus provide evidence that would otherwise have been lost. They can be searched on the NAI site at:

- Census Search Forms
  http://censussearchforms.nationalarchives.ie/search/cs/home.jsp

They can also be searched at Family Search **https://familysearch.org**, and at FindMyPast **http://search.findmypast.com/search-world-records/ireland-census-search-forms-1841-and-1851**.

For a general discussion of the census, written for local historians, but also of use to genealogists, see:

- Crawford, E.M. *Counting the people: a survey of the Irish censuses 1813-1911.* Four Courts Press, 2003.

Census Substitutes: Griffith's Valuation

For the nineteenth century, in the absence of census returns, there are two major sources which can be used to identify heads of households. These are the records of Griffith's Valuation, and the Tithe Applotment books. The originals of both of these sources are held by the Irish National Archives, and (for Northern Ireland) PRONI. The websites of both of these institutions have useful introductions. See also Grenham. Numerous other relevant websites are listed in *IFHoW*; the major ones are noted below.

Between 1848 and 1864, Sir Richard Griffith conducted a valuation of all Irish land in order to determine liability to pay poor rates. The valuation provides details of rural land and town properties including the names of the owners and occupiers and information about the nature and quality of the land. These records are an invaluable aid to identifying the townlands and civil parishes in which our ancestors lived. NAI holds some of the records originally used in the compilation of the valuation, which was subsequently printed in 300+ volumes. A transcript of the printed valuation can be searched for free at:

- Ask about Ireland: Griffith's Valuation
  www.askaboutireland.ie/griffith-valuation

Digitised images from the printed volumes are also available; these can be searched for a fee at:

- Find your ancestors in Griffith's Valuation 1847-1864
  www.findmypast.com/articles/world-records/full-list-of-the-irish-family-history-records/census-land-and-substitutes/griffiths-valuation

Another collection of digitised images is available at:

- Ireland, Griffith's Valuation, 1847-1864
  search.ancestry.co.uk/search/db.aspx?dbid=1269

Valuation information concerning older valuations for the Republic from the mid-1850s until the early 1990s is also available from The Valuation Office; for details, visit:

- Valuation Office: Archives, Genealogy and Public Office
  www.valoff.ie/en/Archives_Genealogy_Public_Office

Census Substitutes: Tithe Applotment Books

The Tithe Applotment Books were compiled between 1823 and 1838. The land in each civil parish was surveyed in order to determine how much tithe should be paid. Tithe was a tax on agricultural land, imposed to support Church of Ireland clergy. Books listing tithe-payers and quantities of land were compiled for most parishes sometime between the years 1823 and 1838. These books only cover rural areas, not towns and cities. They have been digitised, and are searchable on two websites:

- The Tithe Applotment Books
  http://titheapplotmentbooks.nationalarchives.ie
- Ireland Tithe Applotment Books, 1814-1855
  https://familysearch.org/search/collection/1804886

Other Lists of Names

A variety of other name lists are available. Numerous fragments of tax lists, muster rolls, and other census-type listings survive in the repositories listed below (p.10-11). Some of the more substantial are listed here by date. Others are identified by Grenham and by Maxwell; they are also listed in the county guides published by Flyleaf Press (see below, p.XXX).

Pender's Census, 1659

This census records the names of those with title to land, together with the numbers of English and Irish in each townland, and the major Irish surnames in each barony. A number of counties are omitted.

- Pender, Séamus, ed. *A Census of Ireland, 1659, with supplementary material from the Poll Money Ordinances (1660-1661).* H.M.S.O., 1939. Digitised at **www.irishmanuscripts.ie/digital/censusofireland1659/files/html5/ index.html**

Protestant Householders, 1740

The Irish Parliament ordered a census of protestant householders to be taken in 1740. Some returns for Northern Ireland survive, and are indexed at

- PRONI: Name Search
  www.nidirect.gov.uk/information-and-services/search-archives-online/name-search

Religious Census 1766

This lists some 11,000 heads of households, mostly in Northern Ireland, and is searchable (for a fee) at:

- Ireland 1766 Religious Census
  http://search.ancestry.co.uk/search/db.aspx?dbid=5990

For Northern Ireland, see also PRONI's Name Search database just mentioned.

Dissenters Petitions 1775

Numerous Presbyterian dissenters petitioned Parliament in 1775 against their exclusion from voting at vestry meetings. For Northern Ireland, their names are indexed on PRONI's Name Search database.

Irish Flax Growers 1796

In 1796, the government offered a bounty in order to encourage the production of flax. Over 60,000 people applied for this bounty; a list of their names is held by Belfast's Linen Hall Library, and is indexed at:

- Irish Flax Growers, 1796
  www.failteromhat.com/flax1796.php

Irish Rebellion 1798

The names of over 2,000 rebels, plus 6,000 people who placed claims for damages, are listed by:

- Cantwell, Ian. *The 1798 Rebellion: Claimants and Surrenders.* Irish Records Index 6. CD. Eneclann, [20—]

Tithe Defaulters, 1831

As already noted, all occupiers of land had to pay tithe to support Church of Ireland clergy, regardless of their religion. In 1831, many tithepayers went on strike and refused to pay. South-Eastern Ireland was particularly affected. Defaulters' names are listed by:

- McCormac, Stephen. *The 1831 Tithe Defaulters.* Irish Records Index, 4. CD. Eneclann, [20—]. This is also available at Find My Past.

William Smith O'Brien Petition, 1848-9

Following the rising of 1848, some 80,000 people petitioned for clemency for the rebel leader. Their names can now be searched at:

- William Smith O'Brien Petition, 1848-9
  www.findmypast.com/articles/world-records/full-list-of-the-irish-family-history-records/military-service-and-conflict/william-smith-obrien-petition-1848

Landowners Census 1876

The British government ordered a census of everyone who owned more than one acre of land to be taken in 1873. The census was published in 1876, although most of it was compiled in 1874 and 1875. The full text is available on a number of free and commercial websites, listed by *IFHoW*. It is fully digitised at:

- Land Owners in Ireland 1876
  www.failteromhat.com/lo1876.htm

Ulster Covenant 1912
This was signed by c.500,000 Ulstermen, whose names are indexed by:
- About the Ulster Covenant
  www.nidirect.gov.uk/articles/about-ulster-covenant

World War I, 1914-18
The names of some 49,000 Irish soldiers who lost their lives during the First World War were published in 8 volumes in 1923, and are re-published on CD in:
- Committee of the Irish National War Memorial. *Ireland's Memorial Records: World War 1 1914-1918*. CD. Eneclann, [20—].

Their details may also be found on the Commonwealth War Graves Commission database; visit:
- Commonwealth War Graves Commission
  www.cwgc.org

National Register 1939
When the Second World War broke out in 1939, it was necessary to issue identity cards and ration books, and to identify those liable to serve in the armed forces. This only applied in Northern Ireland, since Eire did not take part of the war. In order to undertake these tasks it was necessary to compile a national register of the entire population. This register is now held by PRONI, and is described by:
- Northern Ireland's 1939 National Register
  www.irish-genealogy-toolkit.com/1939-national-register.html

Estate Records & Deeds
The great majority of the Irish population in the eighteenth and nineteenth centuries were small tenant farmers on large estates. Records of tenancies were maintained by these estates, or by the middlemen who sub-let them. These records may include leases, rentals, accounts, surveys, ejectment books (recording details of tenants ejected from their holdings), and other miscellaneous documents. These are unsystematic sources, and may be difficult to search – but they may also provide much more information than other sources. Many estate records have been deposited in NAI, NLI, and PRONI. Their websites (see above, p.XXX) provide further information.

The Dublin Registry of Deeds **www.prai.ie/registry-of-deeds-services** dates from 1708, and records many land transactions since that date (although registration was not compulsory). If your ancestor bought or sold property, details may be recorded here. Many marriage settlements, wills, and other agreements and contracts are registered. It was originally used by protestant landowners to register lands confiscated from Roman Catholics, and to obtain secure title. Smaller landowners gradually began to use it, and, after Catholic emancipation, so did Roman Catholics. About 600,000 deeds were registered prior to 1832; these record at least 2,400,000 names. Many more have since been added. The Registry is particularly useful for the early nineteenth century, by which time registration had become fairly widespread; other sources for that period are scarce. The documents registered included leases, marriage settlements, mortgages, wills (see below, p31-3), and a variety of other documents.

It is not easy to search the Deeds Registry, or to understand the legalese in some of the documents. Bear in mind, too, that only a small percentage of the population would have had cause to use the Registry: most Irishmen were not landowners. However, if persistence in searching these records pays off, the reward may be considerable.

There is an official online index to registrations since 1970. The Memorial books and manuscript indexes have been microfilmed for the Family History Library **https://familysearch.org**. A project is currently well under way to create an online index to earlier entries in the register; see:

- Registry of Deeds Index Project Ireland
  http://freepages.genealogy.rootsweb.ancestry.com/~registryofdeeds

For a detailed discussion of the Deeds Registry, see Grenham. A briefer guide is provided by:

- Registry of Deeds for Family History
  http://irishdeedsindex.net/guides/beginning_research.php

An older source of information is provided by the early seventeenth century Irish patent rolls, which recorded grants of land, as well as a variety of other matters affecting inheritance. The rolls were lost in 1922, but had been calendared before then. See:

- *Irish patent rolls of James I: facsimile of the Irish Record Commission's calendar prepared prior to 1830.* Irish Manuscripts Commission, 1966.

The Plantation of Ulster in the early seventeenth century is well documented. The names of the settlers (mainly Scottish Presbyterians) are recorded in four surveys conducted by the government, one of which is transcribed in:

- Hill, George, ed. *The Plantation in Ulster at the Commencement of the Seventeenth Century 1608-1620.* McCaw, Stevenson & Orr, 1877. Digitised at **https://archive.org**.

Many records relating to the settlement of Londonderry by the Companies of London are now in PRONI. See:
- *Guide to Records of the Irish Society and the London Companies.* PRONI, 1994.

Other Londonderry records are held by London Metropolitan Archives; for example, a 1639 volume identifying planters has been digitised at:
- The Great Parchment Book of the Honourable Irish Society **www.greatparchmentbook.org**

More recently, the Encumbered Estates Court was established in 1849 (succeeded by the Landed Estates Court in 1853) to sell land encumbered by debt after the Great Famine. Between 1839 and 1857 over 3000 estates were sold. Printed rentals and particulars of sale were issued before sales took place, and provide very detailed information concerning tenants and holdings. Records are in NAI and PRONI, and have been indexed by:
- Landed Estates Court Rentals 1850-1885 **www.findmypast.com/articles/world-records/full-list-of-the-irish-family-history-records/census-land-and-substitutes/landed-estates-court-rentals-1850-1885**

Even more recently, the Irish Land Commission was established in 1881 to enable small tenants to purchase their lands, and to assess fair rents. Its records include almost as much information about tenants as they do about landlords. They are now held in NAI and PRONI; at PRONI they are held with the Land Registry archives.

Another way to find out about the Commission's activities is to consult newspapers (see below, p.34-5). They frequently carried detailed reports about the judgements made by its Land Courts, including details of the tenants affected.

Wills and Probate

Wills may be the only documents you can find that were actually written by, or at the direction of, your ancestors. They are likely to name spouses and all surviving children. Since 1858, grants of probate (for the execution of wills) and letters of administration (for intestate estates) have been granted by the Probate Court (until 1877) and the High Court (since 1877). There were eleven district registries, together with the Principal Registry in Dublin. Grants made by these courts were listed in annual calendars. Local registries also made copies of wills before (after 20 years) sending the originals to the Principal Registry (where they were lost in the 1922 fire; only post 1904 Principal Registry wills survive). Despite the destruction, the calendars provide some useful information, including dates, addresses, and occupations. See:

- Calendars of Wills and Administrations 1858-1920
  www.willcalendars.nationalarchives.ie/search/cwa/home.jsp

This page also provides information on searching wills, 1922-82. Copies of wills made by the District Registries are available on microfilm at both NAI and PRONI. Northern Ireland will calendars 1858-1965 can be viewed on a PRONI database, which also provides digitised images of will copies from the District Probate Registries of Armagh (1858-1918), Belfast (1858-1909), and Londonderry (1858-1899). See:

- PRONI: Search Will Calendars
  www.nidirect.gov.uk/services/search-will-calendars

Before 1858, most wills were proved in ecclesiastical probate courts. Diocesan Consistory courts had probate responsibility for testators whose property lay wholly within their own areas. The Prerogative Court had responsibility where property lay in more than one diocese. Sadly, most records of these courts were lost in 1922. However, before the destruction many wills had been copied, and most had been indexed. NAI and PRONI hold numerous transcripts. Those at NAI have been indexed by:

- Index of Irish Wills 1484-1858
  www.findmypast.co.uk/articles/world-records/full-list-of-the-irish-family-history-records/life-events-birth-marriage-death/index-of-irish-wills-1484-1858

Published indexes to the destroyed wills (which, again, may include useful information despite the destruction) include:

- Vicars, Arthur. *Index to the Prerogative Wills of Ireland. 1536-1810.* Dublin: Edward Ponsonby, 1897. (available at **https://archive.org**). For the period 1810-57, the NAI has a manuscript index.
- Phillimore, W.P.W., & Thrift, Gertrude. *Indexes to Irish wills, 1536-1858.* 5 vols. Phillimore & Co., 1909-20. Reprinted Baltimore: Genealogical Publishing Co., 1970. v. 1. Ossory, Leighlin, Ferns, Kildare. v. 2. Cork and Ross,

Cloyne. v. 3. Cashel and Emly, Waterford and Lismore, Killaloe and Kilfenora, Limerick, Ardfelt and Aghadoe. v. 4. Dromore, Newry and Mourne. v. 5. Derry and Raphoe.
- *Indexes to Dublin Grant Books and Wills, 1270-1800.* Reprinted Baltimore: Genealogical Publishing, 1997.

These indexes are available in libraries; they are also available on a variety of different websites (listed in *IFHoW*). For Northern Ireland, both the published indexes, and transcripts held by PRONI, can be searched online at:
- PRONI: Name Search
  www.nidirect.gov.uk/information-and-services/search-archives-online/name-search

There are a variety of other sources of wills. Some 9000 World War I soldiers' wills have been digitised by the NAI **http://soldierswills.nationalarchives.ie/search/sw/about.jsp**. Some Irish wills were proved in the Prerogative Court of Canterbury, and have been digitised by TNA (class PROB 11); these can be searched at **http://discovery.nationalarchives.gov.uk**. The Inland Revenue in London kept registers and indexes of wills and administrations for death duty purposes; the indexes cover the period 1828-79, although the registers survive for most of the period 1828-39 only. They are now held by NAI. Many will transcripts are held by the Genealogical Office (see above, p.10). Copies of 1,370 wills made for estate duty purposes in London, 1812-57, are now in PRONI. Wills in the Deeds Registry have already been mentioned; for these, see:
- Eustace, P. Beryl, et al, eds. *Registry of Deeds, Dublin: Abstracts of Wills.* 3 vols. Stationary Office for the Irish Manuscripts Commission, 1956-84. v.1. 1708-1745. v.2. 1746-85. v.3. 1785-1832. Also available online at: **www.irishmanuscripts.ie/servlet/Controller?action=digitisation_backlist**

For a useful guide to sources for wills, see:
- Ireland Probate Records
  https://familysearch.org/wiki/en/Ireland_Probate_Records

Many other relevant websites are listed by *IFHoW*. Numerous books can be identified in Grenham.

Freeholders Books, Pollbooks, and Electoral Registers
Between 1727 and 1793, only Protestant freeholders possessing land valued at more than forty shillings per annum were entitled to vote. Between 1793 and

1829, the right was extended to Roman Catholics. After 1829, the franchise was even more restricted, being extended only to those possessing land worth more than £10 per annum. Those entitled to vote were listed in freeholders' books; those who actually cast their vote were recorded in pollbooks. Pre-1840 freeholders in Northern Ireland can be searched at:

- About Freeholders Records
  www.nidirect.gov.uk/articles/about-freeholders-records

Lists of those entitled to vote also frequently appeared in late eighteenth and early nineteenth century newspapers (see below). Bear in mind that only a small percentage of the population were entitled to vote.

A Parliamentary inquiry into fictitious votes in 1837-8 listed all those who had been entitled to vote in 1832. Their names are indexed in:

- Reports From Committees, Fictitious Votes (Ireland), Select Committee On Fictitious Votes, 1837-1838
  **http://search.findmypast.co.uk/search-world-records/
  reports-from-committees-fictitious-votes-ireland-select-committee-on-
  fictitious-votes-1837-1838**

An act of 1832 required printed electoral registers to be issued annually. Those for 1885 for the whole of Ireland can be searched at:

- Ireland, Electoral Registers 1885-1886
  **http://search.findmypast.com/search-world-records/
  ireland-electoral-registers-1885-1886**

There are extensive collections of poll books and electoral registers at NAI, NLI, and PRONI, although none has a complete set.

Newspapers

Newspapers are invaluable sources for genealogical information, especially their notices of births, marriages and deaths, and their obituaries; their reports of social events, accidents, court proceedings, inquests, and other matters may also be useful. The major repository of Irish newspapers is the British Library. Its website includes a list of Irish newspapers on the Internet:

- British Library Help for Researchers: Newspapers and Comics
  www.bl.uk/reshelp/findhelprestype/news/index.html

In Ireland, the most substantial collection of newspapers (although far from being comprehensive) is held by NLI. It is currently digitising its collection; the resultant database can be searched at:

- Newspaper Database
  www.nli.ie/en/catalogues-and-databases-printed-newspapers.aspx

Many Irish newspapers have been digitised by:
- Irish News Archive
  www.irishnewsarchive.com
- Irish Newspapers
  http://search.findmypast.co.uk/search/irish-newspapers

Marriage entries in one early newspaper are indexed by:
- Ireland, Marriages in Walker's Hibernian Magazine, 1771-1812
  http://search.ancestry.co.uk/search/db.aspx?dbid=9141

Many other newspaper websites are listed in *IFHoW*. For more information, see Grenham.

Poor Law Records

The relief of poverty in Ireland in the late nineteenth and early twentieth century was provided for by the Irish Poor Law Act, 1838, which was heavily influenced by the English New Poor Law Act of 1834. The 1838 act divided Ireland into 130 poor law unions (there were some subsequent boundary changes), each governed by a board of guardians, and each with a workhouse at its centre. The system was originally designed to accommodate 1% of the population, but by 1851 almost 4% had been driven into workhouses. The aim was only to provide relief to those who were prepared to enter the workhouse.

Many surviving Poor Law Union records are deposited in NAI and PRONI. Records have also been deposited in some local libraries and archive repositories. They date from the period 1838 to 1948. Later records may be closed for privacy reasons. Minute books (which record the names of paupers for a variety of reasons, for example, failure to comply with rules, or absconding), have a good survival rate at NAI. For many Unions, few other records survive; however, in a number of cases, surviving records are very extensive, and may include not just the minute books, but also indoor registers giving the names and personal details of paupers entering the workhouse, registers of Workhouse births and deaths, and other documents. For an introduction to the records, see:
- NAI Research Guides and Articles: Guide to the Records of the Poor Law
  www.nationalarchives.ie/research/research-guides-and-articles/
  guide-to-the-records-of-the-poor-law

For Northern Ireland, PRONI holds the records of 28 poor law unions. They are similar to those held by NAI, bur perhaps more extensive. See:
- PRONI: Frequently Asked Questions: Workhouse Records
  www.nidirect.gov.uk/publications/your-family-tree-series-
  information-leaflet-13-poor-law-records

An extensive guide to Irish workhouses, including full details of surviving records (with some transcriptions), is provided by:
- The Workhouse in Ireland
  www.workhouses.org.uk/Ireland

Dublin workhouses were amongst the busiest in the country. Over 1,500,000 names are recorded in:
- Dublin Workhouses Admission & Discharge Registers 1840-1919
  http://search.findmypast.ie/search-world-Records/
  dublin-workhouses-admission-and-discharge-registers-1840-1919

Trade Directories

Tradesmen, the middle classes, and the gentry are frequently recorded in trade directories of the nineteenth and twentieth centuries; the modern equivalent is the phone book. Only the lowest classes – labourers, small tenant farmers, and servants – are likely to be excluded. Some directories covered the entire country; others were devoted to particular counties or towns. It is easy to use them to check a name or address, to identify the occupiers of particular properties, to trace the locations of particular surnames, or to compare them with information from other sources. However, note that the information in them was usually at least six months out of date before they were published. Bear in mind too that early nineteenth-century directories are much less inclusive than the later so-called *Post Office* directories.

The best collection of Irish directories is held by NLI. Most reference libraries hold directories relating to their own areas. Many have been digitised, and are available on the internet. For a useful introduction, see:
- Irish Ancestors: Directories
  www.johngrenham.com/browse/retrieve_text.php?text_contentid=77

Many directories are digitised at Find My Past **www.findmypast.ie**; some can also be found at World Vital Records **www.worldvitalrecords.com**, and on other database hosts. For Belfast directories, visit Lennon Wylie **www.lennonwylie. co.uk**. An extensive listing of trade directory websites is provided by *IFHoW*.

Occupational Sources

If you know the occupation that an ancestor followed, you may be able to trace information about him through occupational records. Employers' personnel records, the archives of trade unions and professional societies, educational sources, licencing records, and published works such as biographical dictionaries, trade directories, and company histories, may all yield information. Numerous occupational websites are listed by *IFHoW*; many books are listed by Grenham. For some examples of the various different sources available, see:

Apothecaries
- Return of Persons examined and certified as Qualified by Apothecaries' Hall in Dublin, and Number of Prosecutions, 1791-1829
  www.dippam.ac.uk/eppi/documents/10244/page/226615

Architects
- Loebor, Rolf. *A biographical Dictionary of architects in Ireland, 1600-1720*. John Murray, 1981.

Clergy
The *Irish Catholic Directory* was published annually from 1836, and lists priests by diocese and parish. A number of issues have been digitised at **http://babel.hathitrust.org** and elsewhere on the internet.

Lawyers
- Keane, Edward, Phair, P.Beryl, & Sadleir, Thomas U., eds. *Kings Inn Admission Papers, 1607-1867*. Irish Manuscripts Commissin, 1982. Viewable online at **www.irishmanuscripts.ie/servlet/Controller?action=digitisation_backlist**

Medics
- Irish Medical Directory 1872
  www.familyrelatives.com/search/search_irish_medical_directory1872.php

Police
The Royal Irish Constabulary was created in 1836. Its records, which include registers of officers, are in TNA, class HO 184. There are also pension records in PMG 48. For details, visit:
- Royal Irish Constabulary Records
  www.nationalarchives.gov.uk/help-with-your-research/research-guides/royal-irish-constabulary

See also:

- Herlihy, Jim. *The Royal Irish Constabulary: a short history and genealogical guide with a select list of medal awards and casualties.* New ed. Four Courts Press, 2016.

Soldiers and Militia Men

Before Irish independence, a considerable proportion of the British Army consisted of Irish soldiers. Most records are now in TNA, whose Research Guides **http://nationalarchives.gov.uk/help-with-your-research/research-guides-keywords** provide much useful information. All officers are recorded in the *Army list*, which has been published at least annually since 1740. World War I soldiers' wills, and the Commonwealth War Graves Commission, have already been mentioned. A variety of other World War I sources can be searched at

- World War I (1914-1918)
  www.ancestry.co.uk/cs/uk/world-war-1

A number of earlier sources can be searched at:

- British Army Service Records 1760-1915
  http://search.findmypast.ie/search-world-Records/british-army-service-records-1760-1915

In the nineteenth century and earlier, all Irish adult males were liable to serve in the Militia, which was recruited by parish constables. Militia muster rolls for the period 1793-1876 are in TNA, class WO 13. These are arranged by county, and give names, ages, and parishes. Maxwell has a list of earlier muster lists.

Students

- Trinity College, Dublin: Student Records: Entrance records 1637-1961
  www.tcd.ie/Library/manuscripts/collections/genealogy.php

Teachers

- Corcoran, T.S. *Some lists of Catholic lay teachers and their illegal schools in the later penal times.* M.H.Gill & Son, 1932.

Migration Records

Between 9,000,000 and 10,000,000 Irishmen have emigrated since 1700. That is more than the total population of Ireland in the 1840s. Those who could afford it went to America. The poorest went to England, and especially Liverpool. Irish convicts accounted for a substantial proportion of Australia's earliest settlers, and helped to create 'strine', the Australian dialect. Emigration was particularly high during the famine years of the 1840s. In 1890, 40% of those born in Ireland were living abroad, and today no less than 36,000,000 Americans claim Irish descent. Numerous publications relating to Irish emigration are listed by Grenham.

A huge number of websites are devoted to Irish passenger lists, immigration records, convict transportation registers, and the like. Many are listed by *IFHoW*. A few of the largest databases are identified below. The Latter Day Saints Family History Library provides a useful online guide to:

- Ireland Emigration and Immigration
  https://familysearch.org/wiki/en/Ireland_Emigration_and_Immigration

Passenger lists are likely to identify ports of departure and accompanying family members. Everyone who departed for non-European destinations from an English or Irish port between 1890 and 1922, and from ports in Northern Ireland and England between 1922 and 1960, is listed by Board of Trade returns, now in TNA, class BT27, and digitised by:

- Passenger Lists Leaving UK 1890-1960
  http://search.findmypast.co.uk/search-world-records/
  passenger-lists-leaving-uk-1890-1960

Over 17,000 passenger lists, including many from Ireland, have been transcribed at:

- Immigrant Ships Transcription Guild
  http://immigrantships.net

See also:

- The Ships List
  www.theshipslist.com

Passenger lists held by PRONI are listed by:

- Emigration Series
  www.nidirect.gov.uk/articles/emigration-series

A variety of records relating to emigration are held by TNA. These are listed by Maxwell, who also lists records held by PRONI. For records at TNA, see also:

- How to Look for Records of Emigrants
  www.nationalarchives.gov.uk/help-with-your-research/
  research-guides/emigrants

The majority of records relating to Irish emigration are held in the countries where they settled. Overseas records of civil registration and the census are particularly important, but cannot be dealt with here in detail. Brief details are given by both Grenham and Maxwell. Many genealogical guides have been published for specific countries; a few are mentioned below. These are likely to provide more detailed advice.

England
Millions of Irishmen have emigrated to England down through the centuries. Civil registration in England began in 1837, and records the same information as that in Irish records (above, p.15-18). Indexes to the UK GRO registers are available on a number of websites, but most can be freely viewed at:
- Free BMD
  www.freebmd.org.uk.

Certificates have to be ordered from:
- General Register Office
  www.gro.gov.uk/gro/content

Alternatively, they can be ordered from District Registrars. As in Ireland, their indexes are quite different to those of the GRO. Many can be located via:
- UKBMD: Births, Marriages and Deaths and Censuses on the Internet
  www.ukbmd.org.uk

Irish emigrants in England can also be identified in nineteenth-century census returns, which are available on many commercial websites, and are described by:
- Raymond, Stuart A. *The Census 1801-1911: a Guide for the Internet Era.* Family History Partnership, 2009.

The authoritative guide to English genealogy is:
- Herber, Mark. *Ancestral trails: the complete guide to British genealogy and family history.* Rev. ed. Sutton / Society of Genealogists, 2004.

Australia
Many Irishmen were transported as convicts to Australia between 1787 and 1867. Convict records now held in several Australian state archives have been indexed for:
- Convict Records of Australia
  www.convictrecords.com.au

For transportation records held by NAI, together with a transportation database, visit:

- Ireland-Australia transportation records (1791-1853)
  **www.nationalarchives.ie/genealogy1/genealogy-records/
  ireland-australia-transportation-records-1791-1853**

Australian census and civil registration records prior to Federation in 1901 were kept by the individual states. The standard guide to Australian genealogy is:

- Vine Hall, N. J. *Tracing your family history in Australia : a national guide to sources.* The author, 2002.

North America
A detailed guide to passenger lists online is provided by:

- Irish Passenger Lists Research Guide: Finding Ship Passenger Lists and Immigration Records, Ireland to America: A Bibliography of Books, CD-Roms, Microfilm and Online Records
  www.genealogybranches.com/irishpassengerlists

Millions of Irishmen migrated through New York between 1820 and 1957. Between 1855 and 1890, Castle Garden served as an immigration processing station; Ellis Island served the same function between 1892 to 1954. Arrivals at both places can be searched at:

- New York, Passenger Lists, 1820-1957
  http://search.ancestry.co.uk/search/db.aspx?dbid=7488

Some of the Irish records on this database, together with others from Boston, Baltimore, New Orleans, and Philadelphia, are available free at:

- Irish Emigration Database
  www.dunbrody.com/get-involved/irish-emigration-database

For records of Irish immigration to Canada, visit:

- Library and Archives Canada: Immigration Records
  **www.bac-lac.gc.ca/eng/discover/immigration/immigration-
  records/pages/introduction.aspx**

Millions of migrants, including many from Ireland, are listed by:

- Filby, P.W., & Meyer, M.M. *Passenger and immigration lists index: a guide to published arrival records of about 500,000 passengers who came to the United States and Canada in the 17th, 18th, and 19th centuries*. 3 vols. Gale,

1981. This is continued by annual supplements. These volumes index the publications listed in: Filby, P.W. *Passenger and immigration lists bibliography 1538-1900: being a guide to published lists of arrivals in the United States and Canada.* 2nd ed. Gale, 1988.

Many Irishmen who caught ship from America to Ireland are listed by:
- Maher, James P. *Returning Home: Transatlantic Migration from North America to Britain & Ireland 1858-1870.* Irish Records Index 5. CD. Eneclann, [20—].

For a general guide to American genealogy, see:
- Szucs, Loretto Dennis, & Luebking, Sandra Hargreaves. *The Source: A Guidebook to American Genealogy.* Ancestry Publishing, 2006.

For Canada, see:
- Irvine, Sherry, & Obee, David. *Finding your Canadian Ancestors.* Ancestry Publishing, 2007.

Other Miscellaneous Sources

Catholic Qualification Rolls
Under the Catholic Relief Act 1778, Catholics were permitted to lease property, provided that they took an oath of loyalty to the Crown at the Assizes. Those who did so were registered in the Catholic Qualification Rolls by name, occupation, address, date and place of taking the oath. The rolls were lost in the 1922 destruction, but an index to them survives in NAI.

Convert Rolls
Early modern penal laws prevented Roman Catholics from owning property or serving in various professions. These disabilities led many to convert to Protestantism. Under an act of 1703, the names of converts were enrolled. By 1800, over 5,000 names had been enrolled. They are listed in:
- O'Byrne, Eileen, ed. *The Convert Rolls: the calendar of the convert rolls, 1703-1838.* 2nd ed. Irish Manuscripts Commission, c2005.

Dog Licences
Over 6,000,000 people have taken out dog licences since they were first introduced in Ireland in 1865. Was your ancestor one of them? Find out by searching:

- Ireland Dog Licence Registers
  http://search.findmypast.ie/search-world-Records/

  ireland-dog-licence-registers

The Easter Rising and its Aftermath, 1916-1921

The rebellion of 1916 generated a huge amount of paper. Many thousand names of rebels and others affected by the rising and the subsequent troubles are recorded in the archives of the UK War Office, now in TNA (class WO 35). Court martial registers, individual files, search and raid reports, and internment camp/prison registers, have all been digitised by Find My Past:

- Easter Rising & Ireland Under Martial Law 1916-1921
  http://search.findmypast.co.uk/search-world-Records/

  easter-rising-and-ireland-under-martial-law-1916-1921

Freemasons

Over 300,000 Irish freemasons can be identified in:

- Grand Lodge of Freemasons of Ireland Membership Registers, 1733-1923
  http://search.ancestry.co.uk/search/db.aspx?dbid=60904

Schools

Between 1833 and 1900, the number of pupils in Irish schools increased from c.107,000 to c.500,000. Their details are recorded in school registers and other educational records. For a more detailed overview of these sources, see Maxwell. Sources available in NAI are described by:

- Guides to Sources on National Education Records
  www.nationalarchives.ie/topics/Nat_Schools/natschs.html

For Northern Ireland, see:

- Index to School Collections at PRONI
  www.nidirect.gov.uk/publications/index-school-collections-proni

Numerous school registers, c.1860-1920, including details of pupils, their parents, ages, home addresses, and much other useful information, have been digitised at:

- Ireland National School Registers
  http://search.findmypast.ie/search-world-Records/

  ireland-national-school-registers

Tontines 1773, 1775 & 1777
Governments used tontines to raise a fixed amount of capital, on which they paid a fixed annuity. When an investor died, his annuity was divided between all the other investors; his capital was not repaid, except perhaps to the last surviving annuitant For Ireland, registers of subscribers and nominees, payments books, certificates of deaths and marriages and declarations of identity, letter books and memoranda, survive in TNA, Class NDO 3.

Further Reading
This booklet merely provides a brief introduction to Irish genealogy. More detailed information is provided by:
- Grenham, John. *Tracing your Irish ancestors.* 4th ed. Gill & Macmillan, 2012.
- Maxwell, Ian. *Tracing your Irish ancestors: an essential guide to researching and documenting the family histories of Ireland's people.* Pen & Sword, 2008.
- Stewart, Alan. *My ancestor was Irish.* Society of Genealogists Enterprises, 2012.

Much useful advice is provided by the websites of the national institutions listed above, p.10-11. See also:
- Irish Ancestors
  www.johngrenham.com
- Fianna: Guide to Irish Genealogy
  www.rootsweb.ancestry.com/~fianna
- A Primer in Irish Genealogy / Sean J. Murphy
  http://homepage.eircom.net/~seanjmurphy/epubs/primer.pdf

Flyleaf Press **www.flyleaf.ie** has published guides to tracing ancestors for many Irish counties. See, for example:
- O'Connor, Michael H. *A Guide to tracing your Kerry ancestors.* 2nd ed. Flyleaf Press, 1994.

For Northern Ireland, see:
- Maxwell, Ian. *Tracing your Northern Irish ancestors: a Guide for Family Historians.* Pen & Sword, 2010.

For the general background to Irish history, there is a useful historical dictionary:
- Connolly, S.J, ed. *The Oxford Companion to Irish history.* Oxford University Press, 1998.

Subject Index